Who's the Visitor?

Looking up I couldn't miss him

Looking down he noticed me

What a beautiful bird he was

Sweetly singing on that tree

Fine Design Publishing, Don G. Ford ©2013

Editor, Artist, Author and Storyteller, Don G. Ford

This is expressly a work of Fiction, in case you were unaware of that FACT.

The names, characters, places, and events, are all the work of the author's over-active imagination.

The guy hardly sleeps

Dedication:

This Book is dedicated to readers who enjoy good storytelling; in fiction. The kids will certainly smile when reading it, or having it read to them.

Star at Christmas

Jon headed in the door of his home. To his wife's surprise, he was carrying a five foot fir tree. "Wow! The prettiest tree in the forest, I bet."

"Lindy, I spent the better half of the morning hunting this guy down. The tree lot extended down to the edge of the steam on Mr. Baker's property. That's right were I found it, and I knew it was the one."

"You done well, sweetheart."

"I made coffee and sweet rolls. I also made an egg and sausage quiche. It's coming out of the oven in a minute or two."

"You sure know how to spoil a guy. Jon then landed a warm kiss on Lindy's cheek."

"Okay Jon, I'm enlisting you to help put the decorations on our new tree right after we eat."

"I'm your Huckleberry! I brought you another surprise; open it."

"Wait, shouldn't we put it under the tree?"

"Absolutely not, it goes on top of it."

"You got us a new topper for our tree, didn't you?"

"Yes, that other one was missing a couple lights."

"Thanks, I didn't want to complain about it, but the other one was looking a bit haggard,"

AFTER THE MEAL...

"Thank you, doll, for that great breakfast - as usual. I could eat that same food every morning, but you like surprising me too. That's the other thing I love about you; the way you keep switching things up. There's nothing boring about living with you."

Lindy then landed her own kiss on Jon's forehead. "Nothing too good for my man."

Within the space of a few minutes, all of the decorations were sitting in front of the tree, ready to be placed.

"Jon, will you help me with the lights? I'll hold the one end, while you wrap it around."

"Works for me."

TWO HOURS FLEW BY IN NO TIME ...

"Are you ready for the unveiling?"

Jon pulled the tree topper out of the box. It was a gorgeous yellow star and it sparkled, even without lights.

"It's the most beautiful star I've ever seen. Thank you Jon. Now I know why I decided to keep you around, especially for Christmas." Lindy smiled at him. There was no mistaking that look; those times when the heart speaks loudest.

"Wait until you see it all lit up!

When the topper was added, a big smile took over Lindy's face. "I love it, I really do,"

Watching intently from the other room was Bella, their cat. She usually left the tree alone every year, being the huge lazy cat she was. She hardly every got up unless she absolutely had to.

If a mouse landed squarely on her nose, she would gently swat it off like it was a fly. Bella didn't have an aggressive bone in her body. For some odd reason she decided to sleep behind the tree on the plug wire to the wall. I guess they get some buzz off of it.

In the middle of the night, the cat decided to shift positions and head over closer to the fireplace for more warmth. As she moved from her spot behind the tree, her leg got caught in a tangle of wire. As she tried to jump free, and with a screech, she brought down the tree; waking the whole house up and maybe the neighbors too.

Jon and Lindy sprang from their bed to see what was the matter. No visions of gumdrops this night; only a tree laying over with a few broken ornaments. The tree topper had smashed into a hundred little pieces.

"Why Bella? Why you crazy cat?"

"It's okay Babe, I'll get another one in the morning when the store opens. No real harm done; no one got hurt,

I'm glad to see. I'll just have to get a different one. It was the only one of its kind, and it sold out due to being so popular."

"Bad cat, bad cat, Bella."

"Don't be too hard on her, Honey, remember she's old. It's partly my fault for choosing such a delicate tree topper."

"Okay, Bella, the father of the house let you off this time." Lindy glanced back at Jon with a wink.

"It was only an ornament, and they are always replaceable."

"Yes, but it was special because my guy picked it out."

"Are you starting to tear up? Don't; I'll find another cool one, I promise."

The tree was put back up and all of the unbroken ornaments were placed back on the tree. The topper and only two glass balls had fallen victim to this little crime spree.

A couple of wires were added to attach the tree securely to the wall, to prevent a reoccurrence of this tree tragedy.

"There, let's go to bed, and I'll deal with the rest of this in the morning." With a kiss and a hug, both headed back to sleepy land.

That very morning a bright red cardinal was sitting and singing on a branch of a tree near their house. The window of the living room was open just a crack. Our cardinal hopped down to the sill, and then continued hopping until it was inside the window.

As birds usually do, this beautiful crimson member of nature decided to head for the top of the tree. From here our bird could view everything and everyone in the room. Then its chorus began.

"Jon, wake up! It sounds like there's a bird in our house!" As the two of them walked out into the living room, there to their wondering eyes did appear; a cardinal sitting atop their beautiful fir.

Jon looked straight at Lindy and said, "I couldn't buy you a tree topper this magnificent."

Lindy agreed as they opened wide the window to let him escape, but he didn't appear to be going anywhere soon. Our bird was content to remain there for the next two hours before taking flight.

It was such a delight and both Jon and Lindy couldn't help feeling in the Christmas Spirit as they both hugged each other for a while.

That same morning Jon happened to find the perfect tree topper. It was a bright red cloth cardinal, and very durable the clerk assured him. When it was pressed, it played the same song that was heard earlier that morning.

STAR at Christmas

Don G. Ford

A Welcome Christmas Visitor

Christmas Star
by Don Ford

Far atop a noble green fir
Sat a bird, small and still
The cardinal is its name
It landed on my window sill

The window open just a crack
The bird it made its way inside
So quiet did this bird arrive
In our house no place to hide

It flew atop our Christmas tree
Sitting there it made no sound
Maybe thought the tree its home
It didn't stir or move around

The Christmas star on top
It fell and broke last year
But now we have this visitor
A ruby ornament of cheer.

Author Notes

I have heard stories about some unusual things showing up in a live tree when it gets in the house. I thought I would create my own story visitor.

This **STORY** was written in honor of the song birds in our yard that hardly get any billing (oops), pun not intended.

When I'm in my world of FANTASY. keep your REALITY away from me!

If you couldn't tell, I have a thing for Fiction that I'll pass on to my readers.

ANOTHER FUN HOLIDAY TALE

Christmas in July

"Mother do we have any tracing paper?"

"Maybe, what are you working on?"

"I want to trace all the snowflakes on the window today."

"Susan, need I remind you it is July? It's just not possible for snow to fall in July."

"Mom, it's not snow, but it is snowflakes, and they are all in different colors."

"Colored flakes or not, it just isn't possible to see flakes on a day like today. Plus, they would melt before they ever hit the glass.

"Mom, can't you see them?

"Why are we even discussing the impossible?"

"Because you told me time and again to use my imagination. Is it just kids who imagine or do grownups also make things up?"

"Yes, honey! Sorry I cut you off at the pass. Let's see these flakes of yours."

"See, there are pink, and red, and blue ones too."

The mother was flabbergasted as she took the time to stare at the window, where all of the action was taking place. This was really no different than having a make believe tea party with the tea set her daughter came out with.

"Care for a bit of tea, Mom, while we draw our snowflakes?"

This is where things sort of went off the map. There on the window in front of them were flakes of all different colors and hues. They each stayed for a long time on the glass, giving mother and daughter time to trace them.

"This is just amazing," said Mother. "I decided to play pretend with you today, but now I see it is real; even the tea is."

"Yes, Mother, did you think I'd serve you anything but the genuine article?"

NOTE: There was no rationale for this to happen. It wasn't snowing and there wasn't any tea or even water in the cups. The imagination is a wonderful thing, when allowed like a seed to spring up and grow tall.

Stories can blossom into amazing legends. What begins like a speck of thought can turn a child's life completely around with the help of a bit of humor and laughter.

Many a dad, mom, and child have gone on such adventures without leaving their house.

Holiday Without a Christmas by Don Ford

This may be a muse, but don't be too quick to dismiss the thought. Court cases are popping up every where and the word Christmas is making national news. This piece is meant to be a humor piece and a sobering thought all wrapped up in a pretty package with a big green bow, just in time for Christmas, the Holiday!

It will take a lot of getting use to. Christmas is no longer a recognized holiday.

The decision to ban Christmas was made in the 19th Circus Court of Repeals in the West Coast state of Confusion. The panel of judges heard evidence and claims that basically led to their unanimous decision.

Christmas had outlived its usefulness. It was argued that this particular day had become way too commercialized. When storeowners began bringing Christmas trimmings out in February, it was the last straw that sealed the deal.

The new ruling would rename December 25th as The Holiday. Everyone had been conditioned earlier to say Happy Holidays instead of Merry Christmas, so this had been in the planning stages for some time.

Families would still be meeting for a festive get together with one important change. No longer would it be a day of giving, but rather one of taking. The way the Circus court spelled it out: each person was to go to any store in his or her neighborhood and pick out a gift to take home for himself or herself. This way there would be 'no one left behind' without a gift.

Too many children were going without on Christmas, while others were drenched in gifts galore. So now there is a one person, one gift rule that will be strictly enforced. Anyone caught taking more than one gift would face fines and imprisonment.

The churches that represented the voices of the moral majority could not be reached for comment. Christmas would now be called The Holiday. It would be mainly a time for families to get together, and would be still celebrated as a legal holiday on the American calendar. The merriment and drinking would still continue on Holiday Eve.

The next day on the calendar to be scrutinized for possible changes would be the Easter bunny one – another commercialized fiasco. This will not go down without a fight, what with egg farmers calling in everyday registering their complaints.

NOTE:
Don't take Christ out of Christmas and don't remove Christmas as a Holiday. Only the Grinch is authorized to do such a thing!!!

AN
EVER
GREEN
CHRISTMAS
!!!

(Dedicated to Jesus Christ – Born Savior of the world on Christmas Day) He was born, he died, and he rose again. Why not celebrate his Birth and Coming to Earth of this KING everyday of the year.

Dear family,

This is a reminder of that special Christmas Day, 2008, and another special day over 2000 years ago!

I had to find our tree before it got dark. The shadows were already playing games with me. I knew I had about an hour and everything would go black on me in this small forest. That special choice was out there. The trick was finding it. I could have selected one of the giant trees, and removed five foot of the top, but that would be a waste of a good tree.

After an hour of feverishly scouring the entire area, I had come up with nothing. I would have to go home and face the family. With no tree in tow, my children would go all sad-faced on me. This Christmas was to be special. Johnny was home from the war. Our oldest son had been overseas for the last four years and was home at last. He was ready to get on with the rest of his life and marry his childhood sweetheart, Jill.

As I turned to leave, a glow was seen in the sky. At first I thought it was the moon coming out from behind a cloud where it had been hiding. But instead it was a faint light that had appeared on the edge of the forest. It was starting to feel a bit eerie like an alien abduction, but without the sights and sounds of flying saucers. But to my surprise, it was more like a 'burning bush' encounter.

Standing there before me was this lovely Blue Spruce. Surely, it was a reminder of hope. It had to be the answer to my quest. Six foot tall, it looked like it was being lit by a stage light from behind a curtain. How could such a thing be? But I was not one to look a gift horse in the mouth. I would cut this tree and be on my way.

Something from deep down inside of me was screaming, no! What was this that was welling up within me? I couldn't convince myself to steal this tree from its native home. The setting for this tree was perfect.

I knew what to do! It wouldn't need lights because it was already being illumined by some strange source. Maybe there was phosphorus nearby. It was the same glow that we saw when there were fireflies in the summer.

I decided Christmas would be held right here, on this very spot. My wife Martha loved the woods. It was only a mile from our home, and Johnny had often played here with his friends when he was younger. Not 500 feet from this tree were the remnants of his childhood clubhouse. You could almost read part of the original sign that was hand painted: "No grils alowed". It was built from left over projects I was always working on at the house.

Everyone agreed to be a part of this unique experience. I used a tarp to drag the gifts out on; and I used it to surround the base of the tree. Now the tarp would also be used as the skirting for our new tree. I placed the gifts on the tarp and built a great fire. We roasted some hot dogs and afterward we had s'mores. I loved just eating the toasted marshmallows.

We sang a number of Christmas carols, and when we left to go back home, the tree light began to dim. We remembered to bring flashlights and a lantern. The show was obviously over, no more glow from the tree. We came to celebrate a great day, but now the curtain had fallen.

When I tried to shine the light on the tree, it had somehow vanished. How could this be happening? All I could think was that this was a special tree; and the woods held great meaning for us all. I went back the next day, but no tree. The signs of where we built the fire were there, but still no tree.

I think the forest was calling us to that very spot, to celebrate another memorable day, when the Christ child, God's first born son, would be placed in a humble manger. I never told Martha or the kids what happened that day. It didn't seem worth bothering them with the news. We had our family together this year and got to celebrate in the finest place we could; with all of the memories and with our soldier son; our first born child.

Martha took seriously ill the next year. She lost her battle for life on Mother's Day. Pneumonia had taken its toll on her. Johnny and Jill were married and both asked if they could move in with us. They wanted to help with the raising of the younger siblings. I could hardly say no. That tree was a sign, and now Mom was gone too. But at least we know where she is.

Love,
Tom

Author Notes
A Christmas we would forever remember in the woods.

Holiday thought:
Every year my wife and I celebrate the birthday of Jesus. She bakes a small cake, since it is just the four of us. Merry Christmas and Happy Birthday Jesus!

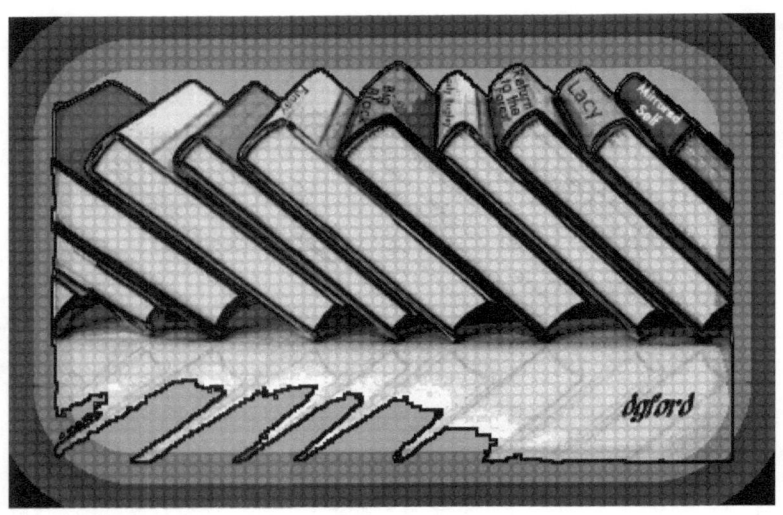

Before you make up your Christmas list, consider a book gift this year. Here are some books for every taste and every age.

Any books requested can be ordered through the author, signed and delivered by mail or, if in the Central N.Y. area, delivered in person. Over all it saves $2 to $3 each book in extra handling and mailing fees. Purchase through Pay Pal at drewsdad13104@yahoo.com or send

check or money order to Don G. Ford
P.O. Box 121 Manlius, N.Y. 13104 TAX/
included.

See the choices here >
Book Shelf 1

Book Shelf 2

See full list at printer > l4al233

https://www.createspace.com/pub/
simplesitesearch.search.do?
sitesearch_query=Don+G.
+Ford&sitesearch_type=STORE

About the author:

This writer started penning stories at the age of 15. He has numerous short story magazine sales across the U.S., and Europe.

He writes with a down-home flavor. Nature and conservation are popular topics with him. He writes in many genres. Known for his poetry and storytelling, short stories are his favorite form of writing. To date he has sold numerous short stories to magazines across the U.S. and has attained International status now with work in Portugal and Cyprus with connections in 62 other countries.

More About the Author

Profile Information

DON FORD ; AKA

dgford, grassroots08, greywolf

Favorite Quote: "The best writing is rewriting" – E.B. White

This writer loves telling stories. Ask any of his listeners of any age; school to retirement kids at heart. The Environment is a hot button topic, and don't get him going on Bullying, and Teen Suicide. The kids are gonna love his Clay Pond series; you guessed it, it's about pond life. It's time kids set aside their hand-held devices, so they can hold a fishing pole, paddle a boat, or even hug a random tree!

The Old Man
by Don Ford

The blowing, gusty winds do come
Stubborn leaves now fall off trees
Branches then must brace themselves
Fall has long since taken leave

The frightful look of winter
He visits us all draped in snow
As the old man settles in
His coat, our covering, head to toe

It shrouds the once green landscape
In a blanket of pure white
Falls in silence all about
To the child it brings delight

This old man winter's visit
He overstays his welcome
We anxiously await the spring
He runs his course and then some

Dumping tons of snow and ice
He puts on quite a winter show
Holding fast his noble place
As we all chant: "It's time to go"

www.ingramcontent.com/pod-product-compliance
Lightning Source LLC
Chambersburg PA
CBHW030548290526
45786CB00004B/1913